YOUR KNOWLEDGE HAS VALUE

The portrayal of Paris in Ernest Hemingway's writings

Nicole Piontek

Bibliographic information published by the German National Library:

The German National Library lists this publication in the National Bibliography; detailed bibliographic data are available on the Internet at http://dnb.dnb.de.

ISBN: 9783346577795
This book is also available as an ebook.

© GRIN Publishing GmbH
Nymphenburger Straße 86
80636 München

Print and binding: Books on Demand GmbH, Norderstedt, Germany
Printed on acid-free paper from responsible sources.

The present work has been carefully prepared. Nevertheless, authors and publishers do not incur liability for the correctness of information, notes, links and advice as well as any printing errors.

GRIN web shop: https://www.grin.com/document/1168354

RHEINISCHE FRIEDRICH-WILHELMS-UNIVERSITÄT BONN
INSTITUT FÜR ANGLISTIK, AMERIKANISTIK UND KELTOLOGIE

The portrayal of Paris in Ernest Hemingway's writings

Term paper for
Literatures and Cultures in Comparison
Summer semester 2020

Nicole Piontek

Table of Contents

1. Introduction

Hemingway's career as a writer grew during his years in Paris. As part of the Lost Generation he expatriated in the 1920's to the city of freedom. The Lost Generation refers to the post-World War I generation. This generation lost all stability regarding a sense of identity, values like hope, ideals, religion and political believes. Therefore, the traditional value system was lost which led to aimlessness and a sense of drifting through life (cf. "Lost Generation."). Hemingway was in search of stability and a place where he could thrive as an author which he found in Paris. By the time the young writer arrived in Europe, there already was an established American expatriate community in the city which made expatriation much easier for Hemingway. The first chapters of this paper try to recapitulate the development of expatriation to Paris. What were the reasons for people, especially artists, to move to the European city and how did Hemingway himself find his way to Paris?

Furthermore, this paper wants to show how Hemingway represents the city in his writings. As he loved the city and regarded it as his hometown it arouses the interest to see in how far this excitement is visible in his writings. Three different genres will be discussed throughout the analysis to create a balanced overview of the representation of Paris. Hemingway's debut novel *The Sun Also Rises* shows Paris in Hemingway's fiction. The author's memoir *A Moveable Feast* offers a more psychological approach to Paris, whereas a selection of his articles for the Toronto *Star* work as a realistic documentation of life in Paris. What are the differences of the portrayal of Paris in these genres? Is his passion towards the city visible in every work? This paper will also try to answer the question whether Hemingway represents the whole city of Paris or if the author emphasizes on the parts of Paris dominated by the American expatriates, which were mostly on the Left Bank of the Seine.

2. The development of expatriation

Long before Hemingway left America for Paris many others did the same. As Earnest states:

> One of the enduring themes in the literature of the United States is the conflict between American and European values. On the one hand there has been the obvious cultural heritage from the Old World; on the other, the break with many of the old traditions. (Earnest 3)

The first reason for artists leaving America in the 19th century was the absence of institutions for artists of all kinds: "Until after the Civil War there were in the United States no great libraries, no genuine universities, no first-rate instruction in music and art. Political and social conservatives were often appalled at the rapidity of social change in America." (Earnest 4). For Americans to be able to study arts was a long way. Earnest describes the difficult way to being an artist with the example of John Adams' road to art: "He himself [John Adams] needed to study politics and war so that his sons could study mathematics and philosophy, and their children might study painting, poetry, and music." (ibid. 5). Earnest concludes: "However, American artists were not content to accept Adam's delayed timetable." (ibid.). Therefore, the first people started to move to Europe, i.e. Thomas Hutchinson and Edith Wharton (cf. ibid. 4). As there were no schools or other institutions for art in America in the mid-19th century, there was no fine art. The first expatriates wanted to experience this in Europe and tried to bring a more valuable sense for artists back to America. "Emerson said that 'from 1790 to 1820 there was not a book, a speech, or a conversation, or a thought' in Massachusetts. " (ibid. 8). Although Emerson might overexaggerated with this statement, it still highlights the overall atmosphere of American artists in the 19th century. In addition, some of the most important authors like Washington Irving and James Fenimore Cooper expatriated and stayed in Europe for a long time (cf. ibid.) which strengthens the neglect of artists in America.

Nevertheless, these were only the beginnings of expatriation in America, as more and more people left the country until migration climaxed in the 1920's: "Nothing before or since has equalled the mass expatriation of Americans of the 1920's. It has almost the quality of the instinctive migration of the lemmings." (Earnest 251). Among these expatriates where not only artists but all kind of people: young and older people, people with different professional backgrounds i.e. scholars and artists. Most of these people went to France, especially to Paris (cf. ibid). As expatriation already happened years before the 1920's, people now had idols which they honoured and looked up to: "The forerunners they honored were Gertrude Stein, Ezra Pound, and T. S. Eliot." (ibid. 251). Most importantly, Gertrude Stein was a very respected woman whom everyone wanted to meet (cf. ibid. 252). "Thus the three of the seminal figures in twentieth-century American literature were already established in Europe at a time when young writers fresh from the army or from college were beginning their careers." (Earnest 251). Furthermore, artists like James Joyce and Igor Stravinsky lived in Paris. Sylvia Beach opened the bookstore Shakespeare and Company which "[…] quickly became a center for American expatriates, many of whom dropped in daily and had their mail delivered there." (Earnest

251). Americans created an own community in Paris as they "[…] crossed the ocean and colonized the Left Bank of the Seine." (Earnest 252). Paris became a status for itself: "[…] residence in Paris after the war became what a later generation would call an 'in thing'" (Earnest 258).

This high number of expatriates is based on the fact that in the 1920's Americans recognized more and more reasons to leave America for Europe. The already established society in Europe and Paris fuelled the overall dissatisfaction of life and civilization in America: "[…] their prolonged apprenticeship in Europe enabled them to view American life from the perspective not only of distance but of adversary cultural values." (Aldridge 116). Americans who had already lived in Paris for years have a new perspective on life in America, which they shared with others and what then led to more people wanting to expatriate to a place with more freedom. To add to this, the aftermath of World War I offered Americans the chief reason for expatriation: "Failure of belief in all of the traditional panaceas (religion, politics, economics, romance) led to the bleak "waste land" atmosphere so evident in T. S. Eliot's poem of that name (1922) or Theodore Dreiser's 1925 novel *An American Tragedy*." (Wagner-Martin 5). The so-called Lost Generation was among the mass expatriation. The loss of the belief in traditional values, which were still cherished in America, led to people seeking a different life with more freedom. Expatriated wanted more privacy and rebelled against American puritanism by moving to France (cf. Earnest 252). Especially artists blamed every problem in America on its "puritan-industrial culture" (cf. ibid 253). Earnest again picks up the notion of America being a cultural wasteland:

> […] the American past was pictured as a cultural wasteland in which wandered a few tragic pioneers […] Somehow or other Poe's alcoholism, Emerson's loss of memory in later life, Stephen Crane's death of tuberculosis, Frank Norris's from peritonitis, became examples of what America did to the literary artists. (Earnest 253)

In Paris people could experience much more freedom. They can consume alcohol, as there is no prohibition. Paris has a much more open sex and love life, i.e. Stein defends lesbianism and unmarried couples are invited to parties just the same as married couples (cf. Earnest 252). Due to the mass of Americans in Paris Field argues that the Left Bank of the Seine is no longer a fully French area: "This is a Paris created by its American inhabitants and defined by main boulevards, particular cafés, and the mores of the expatriates. The result is a cosmopolitan American city unhindered by the restrictions of Prohibition." (Field 31). Furthermore, life in Europe for Americans was cheap, which again offered much more freedom: "Because of the devaluation of European currencies, American dollars often brought a fantastic rate of exchange." (Earnest 256). Expatriates could live a wealthy life in Europe accompanied by much cheaper publishing costs for i.e. magazines in Europe (cf. ibid.): "At home Hemingway had to devote his whole time to newspaper work; as a foreign correspondent in Europe he could live by sending home an occasional report while American magazines consistently rejected his stories." (Earnest 258).

3. Hemingway's way to Paris

"Hemingway's experience is typical." (Earnest 258) regarding his way to a life in Paris in the 1920's. He had visited Paris for the first time when he stayed with his Red Cross volunteer comrades in the city for a few days in 1918. After his return from the war he eventually moved to Chicago in 1920 (cf. Kennedy 81). Here, he met his soon to be wife Hadley and "[...] a lively crowd which included Sherwood Anderson" (ibid.). After Anderson returned to America from his trip to Paris, he talked in detail about the French capitol and its culture: "Anderson planted the idea of going abroad; after returning from a summer visit to France, he regaled Hemingway and his new bride with details of the trip, assuring them, 'the place to go was Paris [...]'" (ibid.). Hemingway was intrigued by Anderson's stories, as he repelled American civilization and its prohibitions: "Almost every aspect of the United States was distasteful to him." (Earnest 259). Wagner-Martin adds: "Like many writers and artists, he objected to the legislation of morals that Prohibition, the resurgence of all-American feeling, and the rebirth of the Ku Klux Klan suggested." (Wagner-Martin 16). Therefore, Hemingway already knew that he wanted to escape life in America, and Anderson showed him a place with more freedom and less prohibitions: "The point is that Hemingway's generation of Americans was the first to approach Europe without the blinders of puritanism." (Earnest 259), which is why Hemingway was part of a generation which could easily leave their hometown, as there were open minded and willing to break American standards. Quickly after their conversation with Anderson, Hemingway and Hadley moved to Paris (cf. Kennedy 83). Hemingway worked as a correspondent for the Toronto Star, but he mainly seeked "[...] to live the life of the expatriate writer and to learn all he could about writing." (Wagner-Martin 3). Thanks to Anderson, who gave them instructions, he soon made friends with the much-honoured Gertrude Stein and numerous writers and artists, i.e. Pound, Fitzgerald, and Henry James (cf. Kennedy 83). This opened many possibilities and led to

4

a comfortable acclimatization in Paris. Hemingway had an easy start in Paris as he immigrated to an already existing community. Therefore, one might not call him a trendsetter or adventurer, as he purely joined a secure city full of Americans (cf. Earnest 252). The couple stayed in Paris until Hadley got pregnant, as they wanted to raise their child in Toronto. Nevertheless, they quickly returned to Paris, because: "[…] prohibition and the puritanism of Toronto disgusted him […]" (Earnest 259).

4. Representation of Paris in Hemingway's writing

4.1. Fiction – The Sun Also Rises

Part of the expatriate life he found there [in Paris] is reflected in his first full-length novel, *The Sun Also Rises* – a life of drifting from bar to bar, of sexual promiscuity, of going to Spain for bullfights. (Earnest 259)

The Sun Also Rises offers various descriptions of Paris which lead to a detailed depiction of the city. The reader experiences the city through countless walks and rides of the protagonist Jake Barnes. Nevertheless, Field states that the novel is not to be considered as a tourist guide but rather a lifestyle-guide for a life in Paris of the 1920's (cf. Field 30). Moreover, Field argues that it not only "[…] offers an insider's perspective on the lifestyle of the self-exiled writers, artists, and bon vivants who made Paris in the 1920s legendary, but also mythologizes the historic moment." (Field 36). Therefore, the novel was granted as a *roman á clef*, which means that it described a part of the life of expatriates in Paris (cf. Field 29). The protagonist Jake Barnes describes some of the most important places for American expatriates in Paris, which include: "[…] the importance of cafés and bars such as the Dôme, Select, Closerie des Lilas, Deux Magots, Zelli's, Café Napolitain, The Crillon, and The Ritz." (Field 33). Although Hemingway creates a Paris in *The Sun Also Rises* which is similar to the real city, the setting is still a constructed and slightly altered place and is only roughly based on the real Paris. Aldridge argues that the representation of Paris is not a realistic one: "[The novel is] not a realistic reflection of a world but the literal manufacture of a world, piece by piece, out of the most meticulously chosen and crafted materials." (Aldridge 123). Nevertheless, the setting fits perfectly to the attitude of its characters: "Paris is ideal. Its cosmopolitanism, its café culture, its tolerance of difference, its respect for the creative mind and arts, its joie de vivre." (De Roche 146). Also, the existence of almost entirely non-French characters fit to the very Americanized city (cf. Reynolds, "The *Sun* in Its Time" 49) which Hemingway tries to compensate with

5

the usage of numerous French words like *poule, bal musette* and *fine á l'eau*; as well as the detailed enumeration of Parisian streets and places. Through this the author re-establishes credibility and authenticity.

The first description of Paris offers the first paragraph of the third chapter:

> It was a warm spring night and I sat at a table on the terrace of Napolitain after Robert had gone, watching it get dark and the electric signs come on, and the red and green stop-and-go traffic-signal, and the crowd going by, and the horse-cabs clippety-clopping along at the edge of the solid taxi traffic, and the *poules* going by, singly and in pairs, looking for the evening meal. (Hemingway, *The Sun Also Rises* 22)

The paragraph introduces Paris as very lively and one can see a lot of people passing by. Furthermore, electric lights and solid traffic are mentioned which creates a very urban picture. The depiction of Paris being crowded and urban continues throughout the novel in Jake's numerous walks and taxi rides, i.e. "I [...] passed the tables of the Rotonde, still crowded [...]" (ibid. 37) and "The Boulevard was busy with trams and people going to work." (ibid. 43). In addition, the topic of sexuality is quickly introduced: Barnes' attention is on a woman walking up and down the street. As soon as their eyes meet the woman joins Barnes at his table. This woman, Georgette, is a *poule* which means she is a prostitute. Barnes must only look at Georgette to make her join him (cf. ibid.). The easiness of raising the attention and getting the company of a prostitute establishes the depiction of Paris being a permissive city from beginning on. In addition, Georgette is treated equally throughout their journey from the café to a restaurant and the club. She is talking to Barnes' friends as if she is a friend herself. This tolerance and easiness must have been very exotic for the puritan American readers. In addition to the tolerance towards prostitutes comes the tolerance towards homosexuals which is described in the club later. The sexual freedom described in *The Sun Also Rises* correlates with the real Paris in the 1920's: "Paris in the 1920s was a city free of sexual restraint and strict rules about sexual roles." (Caswell 99). Nevertheless, Hemingway hints at an ambivalent awareness of the situation in the city: when Georgette is asked how she liked Paris she answers: "It's expensive and dirty." (ibid. 26) whereas Frances argues: "I find it extraordinarily clean. One of the cleanest cities in all Europe." (ibid.). This shows that Paris is not wonderful and perfect for everyone as Georgette thinks of Paris as dirty due to her profession.

The topic of sexuality recurs in Jake Barnes himself, as he is impotent due to a war wound. Paris offers the protagonist a way to compensate his wound, which is highlighted with him going back and forth from Montparnasse to the Right Bank of the Seine. Kennedy strengthens the existence of a separated Paris in *The Sun Also Rises*. There is the Right Bank, the traditional Paris: "[…] which Hemingway here associates with work, male camaraderie, and (implicitly) an escape from sexuality." (Kennedy 103), and there is the Left Bank which is "[…] known for unconventional eroticism, for its acceptance of homosexuality, bisexuality, promiscuity, perversion, and prostitution." (ibid.). As Jake finds himself again and again in Montparnasse, he there "[…] surrounds himself with sexual activity and romantic intrigue; he comes back to this erogenous zone as if to participate vicariously in the circulation of desire." (Kennedy 103). For instance, Jake Barnes and his friend Robert Cohn meet in a Café on the Left Bank in the end of chapter two (cf. Hemingway, *The Sun Also Rises* 19) and switch to the Café Napolitain on the Right Bank. Here, he meets Georgette, the *poule*, which contradicts Kennedy's assumption of the Right Bank being an escape of sexuality. Still, he quickly goes back to the Left Bank with Georgette (cf. ibid. 23).

Not only sexual freedom but freedom regarding gender roles in Paris is addressed in Hemingway's novel. The character Brett Ashley symbolizes this freedom for the whole female gender in Paris as she can be regarded as a *New Woman*. The *New Woman* was a feminist ideal which demanded equal rights for women and men from the late 19th century up into the 20th century: "In short, the new woman rebelled against patriarchal marriage and, protesting against a social order that was rooted in female biology, she refused to play the role of the ethereal other." (Martin 68). Furthermore, Martin states: "The new woman's radical challenge to the traditional social structure is seen in Lady Brett Ashley, who has stepped off the pedestal and now roams the world." (Martin 68). Brett wears very masculine clothes: "She wore a slipover jersey sweater and a tweed skirt, and her hair was brushed back like a boy's." (Hemingway, *The Sun Also Rises* p. 30) but is still described as feminine and beautiful: "Brett was damned good looking. […] She was built with curves like the hull of a racing yacht, and you missed none of it with that wool jersey." (ibid.). Already Cohn's reaction to Brett beforehand shows how beautiful Brett must be, as he is looking at her as if he saw the promised land (cf. ibid. p. 29). She attracts all attention in the room. Still, her masculine clothes are accompanied by her masculine behaviour: her way of talking, the fact that she drinks a lot of alcohol and the fact that she is dancing with a lot of different men. She is not restricted by any conventional rules. Therefore, she can be regarded as a *New Woman*. In that sense, Brett is a figure of hope for women in the 1920's and simultaneously Paris is depicted as a place where a *New Woman* can live and express herself freely. Nevertheless, the end of the novel demonstrates that her unconventional and non-puritan way of life does not lead her to happiness, as she is just as lost and alienated as her expatriated friends. Earnest strengthens this argument by saying: "[…] American expatriates before the 1920's were still committed to puritan views on sexual morality and the idea that life is a serious business. The hedonism of the expatriates of the twenties is part of the larger context of the era following World War I. Hemingway's Englishwoman, Lady Brett Ashley, is as lost as the Americans she associates with." (Earnest 268).

Moreover, *The Sun Also Rises* creates a rather negative attitude towards tourism:

> By using Cohn, Jake, and Bill as representative Americans in Paris during the expatriate period, Hemingway portrayed the best and worst qualities of Americans abroad. His scathing portrait of American tourists leaves little doubt about his feelings for the huge number of summer visitors who flocked into Paris from 1920 on. (Martin 71)

In chapter five the reader accompanies Jake on his way to work. This passage feels very lightly, and the protagonist is in a good mood: "It was a fine morning. […] All along people were going to work. It felt pleasant to be going to work." (Hemingway, *The Sun Also Rises* 43). Jake Barnes sees a few tourists on his way, but clearly separates himself from them. He regards himself as a Parisian going to work, and not an American visiting the city, as Field points out: "Jake's methodical recounting of street names, cafés, and quartiers underscores his status as an étranger. Yet he is comfortably cosmopolitan in his "home town" of Paris and distinguishes himself from the tourists he passes." (Field 35).

Moreover, Paris' permissiveness is strengthened by the change of settings in *The Sun Also Rises*. When Jake and his friends travel to Spain a big change of atmosphere is visible already in the beginning of their way to Spain:

> For a while the country was much as it had been; then, climbing all the time, we crossed the top of a Col, the road winding back and forth on itself, and then it was really Spain. There were long brown mountains and a few pines and far-off forests of beech-trees on some of the mountainsides. (Hemingway, *The Sun Also Rises* 99).

Spain is introduced as a much more natural setting than Paris. The description quickly intensifies the natural aspects which can almost be depicted as idyllic after the "noisy" chapters in Paris:

[…] and turn out to avoid running into two donkeys that were sleeping in the road. We came down out of the mountains and through an oak forest, and there were white cattle grazing in the forest. Down below there were grassy plains and clear streams, and then we crossed a stream and went through a gloomy little village […] (ibid.).

The detailed description of nature continues while Bill and Jake go fishing (cf. ibid. 122). Furthermore, the mentioning of the two donkeys is a motif for this change of setting as there were no animals mentioned in Paris. Paris was introduced as a purely urban city. In contrast, Spain has not only donkeys, but also places to go fishing. Furthermore, Jake digs for worms just outside the hotel and a goat watches him while he is searching for worms (cf. ibid. 117). Hemingway introduces an idyllic natural setting which contrasts Paris in every way, as Donaldson states: "As almost every commentator on the novel has noticed, the interlude at Burguete stands in idyllic counterpoint to the sophisticated pretentiousness of Paris and the destructive passions of Pamplona." (Donaldson 37). This idyllic fishing trip in nature of Bill and Jake offers a calm break in the story. Not only the scenery becomes a more natural and simpler one, but also Jake's and Bill's actions and dialogues are much more reflective. Although they are still drinking a lot of wine (cf. Hemingway, *The Sun Also Rises* 115 and 126), it is not as excessive as before in Paris. The city Pamplona itself is not as natural and idyllic as the setting of the fishing trip. Already the second sentence after Jake's and Bill's arrival in the city hint at a connection between the Spanish city and Paris: "Out in the plaza they were stringing electric-light wires to light the plaza for the fiesta." (ibid. 135). As previously mentioned, chapter three of the novel introduces electric signs in Paris. This similar description highlights the similarity of the two cities. Furthermore, the group of friends walk around the city, just like Jake did in the beginning of the novel in Paris, and again, through the walk Hemingway describes the city. On the one hand this description offers an introduction to an again livelier scenery. It ends the calm break the reader had through the fishing scene as now the scenery is full of people and "noisy", similar to that in Paris. Also, the usage of alcohol becomes more excessive again as even Cohn gets drunk and they also serve absinthe in Pamplona: "[…] we each ordered an absinthe […]" (ibid. 169). This hints at Pamplona being permissive as well. Nevertheless, there is a difference between Paris and Pamplona. Paris is filled with people and permissiveness, whereas Pamplona is all about the fiesta and bullfighting. Without each Pamplona is a much quieter and more deserted city. Overall, the change of settings offers the reader an outside perspective on Paris, as well as the chance of comparison and henceforth, a more relativized judgement. Still, the effect of the second city in the novel is controversially discussed, as some argue Pamplona

9

turns Paris into a *Waste Land* and others are strengthening its similarities (cf. Stoneback 43).

4.2.   Memoir – A Moveable Feast

Field states: "While A Moveable Feast presents a Paris of memory and nostalgia for Hemingway, The Sun Also Rises is a fictionalized depiction of the Left Bank [...]" (Field 30). Here, Field hints that *A Moveable Feast* is rather based on the psychological effects of a life in Paris than on a description of the city. Hemingway wanted to be known as a hard-working man. Therefore, he repeatedly emphasized his poverty and hunger to strengthen his depiction of a hard-working writer under difficult circumstances. Nevertheless, this depiction is not very realistic as he earned around $ 1,500 as a correspondent. In his article "Living on $ 1,000 a Year in Paris" (which will be discussed in the next chapter), he himself described how cheap life in Paris can be, this contrasts the depiction of his life in Paris in *A Moveable Feast*. In addition, his wife Hadley had a rich trust fund: "Hadley's fortune would be about $ 50,000, which, safely invested, would provide an income of $ 3000 a year. In 1920 the average working man was earning only $ 1342. Three thousand dollars a year was a comfortable income." (Reynolds, *The Young Hemingway* 125). Taverniere-Courbin agrees on this amount of income and on Hemingway not being poor in Paris (cf. Pizer 15). Throughout *A Moveable Feast* Hadley's income is never mentioned. Still, her wealth is described through her support of her husband: "She and he travel together and go to the races together, she is at home with meals when he has finished work, and she is warmly present in bed in the moonlight." (ibid. 21). As Pizer continues this leads back to "Hemingway's anxiety about living on Hadley's money (an almost psychopathic obsession about rich women supporting artists that was to plague him all his life)." (ibid.). In addition, Hemingway grew as a writer in Paris, but he wants to make sure people know that this did not happen in either the touristic area of Paris or "[...] that this growth has not occurred within the context of the expatriate cafés of Montparnasse." (Pizer 9). He wants to make sure that his work is solely linked to him being a hard-working man and not to the advantages a life in Paris offered in the 1920's.

Furthermore, Hemingway is obsessed with the theme of hunger. Especially chapter eight in *A Moveable Feast* offers a wide description of his hunger. He starts with: "You got very hungry when you did not eat enough in Paris [...]" (Hemingway, *A Moveable Feast* 65). Here, he creates a connection between his hunger and the city Paris, as Paris has so many opportunities regarding restaurants and cafés that one cannot ignore any hunger. Hemingway quickly describes the effects his hunger has: "By the time you reached 12 rue de l'Odéon your hunger was contained but all of your perceptions were heightened again. The photographs looked different and you saw books that you had never seen before." (ibid. 66). He links hunger to creativity and the perception of art and the world. He emphasizes the connection of hunger and creativity with the example of the painter Cézanne. Hemingway himself only utterly understands his painting while being hungry and wonders if Cézanne himself was hungry while painting it. He concludes with the thought: "[...] but I thought it was possible only that he had forgotten to eat." (ibid. 65). One might argue that Hemingway wishes to forget his hunger through his writing as well. Still, he seems to be most productive after eating, i.e. towards the end of chapter eight Hemingway talks about hunger and discipline: "It is necessary to handle yourself better when you have to cut down on food so you will not get too much hunger-thinking. Hunger is good for discipline and you learn from it." (ibid 71). His excessive description of hunger and its effects emphasize the fact that he is not only talking about physical hunger. This is also strengthened by the fact that he did not need to suffer from hunger as his wife Hadley had enough money to buy food. Hemingway's hunger is much more an intellectual and emotional one. He is hungry for a good story and good writing. Pizer describes this as follows:

> All these sources of physical, intellectual, and emotional nourishment [i.e. seeking to write truly and well, and a hunger for the books at Shakespeare & Co] help establish what can be called a creative alimentary process. Hunger is assuaged, which produces the capacity of creativity, which is followed by further hunger. (Pizer 15).

Hemingway is not describing a physical hunger but a hunger which results from the search of intellectual and emotional nourishment: "Es ist eine Verbindung von Lebensgier und Arbeitsintensität, eine Art von Besessenheit, die sich aus materieller Beschränkung und emotionaler Befreiung speist." (Daufenbach 297). Overall, Pizer describes the vicious circle from nourishment to creativity: "Sustenance, and of course sustenance not limited to food but rendered most clearly by food, results in the capacity of work, which results in hunger, which – once satisfied – again produces the capacity for work." (Pizer 15). Paris offers the fulfilment of every aspect needed for this circle, and even cheaply. Henceforth, working and being creative in Paris is extraordinarily successful and effective.

The first chapter of the novel introduces the importance of the place an artist is working in. Hemingway starts the novel by describing a bad surrounding: "It was a sad, evilly run café where the drunkards of the quarter crowded together and I kept away from it because of the smell of dirty bodies and the sour smell of drunkenness." (Hemingway, *A Moveable Feast* 15) in which he cannot write his story. He moves to a "[…] pleasant café, warm and clean and friendly […]" (ibid. 17). There, he writes a story about Michigan which he had written several times in the past, but "[…] in one place you could write about it better that in another." (ibid.). With this Hemingway introduces the term *transplanting*, which means that the change of place results in a change of creativity. In Hemingway one can see *transplanting* already in the fact that he expatriated to become more creative in another far-off country. But also, in Paris itself *transplanting* is possible. Paris is described as a good place to do so as it offers numerous different places and surroundings. In *A Moveable Feast* Hemingway merely uses the metro or a taxi to move from different places: "To him, at least in memory, Paris is a city where he reaches his destinations on foot." (Pizer 10). Therefore, Hemingway uses walking for transplanting in his memoir, i.e. by choosing the good café over the bad one which is closer, and with his choice of the Closerie des Lilas and his walk to box with Pound (cf. ibid.). Paris offers artists the freedom and possibility of transplanting:

> It [Paris] is itself an image of freedom in that it harbors – in its quartiers, its residents, and its activities – a sufficient range of life to dramatize how freedom of choice, and therefore, as in transplanting, a fuller growth, lie within one's capacity simply through an act of movement. (Pizer 11).

Lastly, *A Moveable Feast* introduces the topic of sexuality. While writing in the good café, Hemingway speaks of possession: "You [the girl in the café] belong to me and all Paris belongs to me and I belong to this notebook and this pencil." (Hemingway, *A Moveable Feast* 18). He transforms the girl and Paris into art. Therefore, sexual desire goes hand in hand with creativity (cf. Pizer 12). Hemingway creates a Paris of sexual freedom, as he is allowed to desire this young girl in the café: "[…] for expatriates, Paris was above all a world of sexual freedom – a place where the writer could feel desire, could translate (if he or she wished) desire into action, and could write about desire." (Pizer 12). Furthermore, Hemingway strengthens the importance of sexuality for creativity with the portrayal of Gertrude Stein and Fitzgerald. Hemingway argues that both are "[…] lacking in the strength of will necessary to work hard and honestly at their craft, and in both instances he associates this insufficiency in creative energy with sexual weakness." (Pizer 13). For Hemingway Gertrude Stein's sexual weakness is visible in her being homosexual. This correlates with "[...] Hemingway's theme that the American artist in Paris is most successful when he maintains a 'normal' American marriage." (ibid. 21). Still, the possibility to live homosexuality openly in Paris again underlines Paris' freedom.

4.3. Journalism

4.3.1. "Living on $1,000 a Year in Paris"

Hemingway's newspaper article "Living on $1,000 a Year in Paris" was published on February 4, 1922 in The Toronto Star Weekly. He was about 21 years old writing this article. At this time, Hemingway had only spent about one month at a fairly young age in Paris, which is not a long time to explore and understand a whole new city and its culture. Nevertheless, Hemingway advertises Paris as being wonderful and cheap while offering examples which he presumably got from others as he had only lived in Paris for a short time. Still, at that time these detailed examples offered credibility and authenticity as not many Americans and Canadians have been to Europe before.

His article operates as an advertisement for young American and Canadian readers. Paris was known for being expensive. Hemingway tries to shift this impression to show that a life in Europe (especially Paris) is possible and can even be luxury for people earning dollars due to the inflation of European currencies and the resulting exchange rates. He blames the false representation of the city on tourists and their false reports: The city is divided by the river Seine. The right bank is occupied by tourists and is therefore much more expensive than the left bank. He describes this with their encounter with the two girls from New York who stayed at an expensive tourist hotel: "They are now located in a hotel on the left bank of the Seine, where five hundred francs will last two weeks instead of two days [...]" (Hemingway, *Living on $1,000*). The article is also a guide for a luxury life in Paris. Furthermore, he describes the cheapness of wine and beer: "Red wine is sixty centimes a bottle and beer is forty centimes a glass." (ibid.) which refers to Paris' freedom and its exotic culture, as due to the prohibition in the United States of America from 1920 to 1933 all kinds of alcohol were prohibited. By telling that wine and beer is not only available but also cheap in Paris, Hemingway strengthens Paris' freedom.

Hemingway acts as an autodiegetic narrator. As already mentioned, he gains credibility by using detailed and precise examples. For instance, he names exact prizes for their room, breakfast, meals, desserts, alcohol, and transportation. Moreover, he does not use a variety of adjectives. Through this, the most important ones stay in mind: cheap, comfortable, and enjoyable. In the first paragraph he uses a lot of repetitions of the word "cheap", which again strengthens the importance of the adjective and immediately lets the reader know the essence of his article.

Overall, Hemingway creates the image of him being experienced in Paris and an expert on living in Paris. He guides his readers through a luxury and wealthy life in Paris. Paris is therefore portrayed very positively and especially the worth of American money is strengthened. Nevertheless, Hemingway also highlights the existence of mass tourism in Paris and furthermore portrays tourism as something negative, as it is the reason for higher prizes and the alteration of the city scape.

4.3.2. "American Bohemians in Paris"

"American Bohemians in Paris" was published on March 25, 1922 and is therefore still written during Hemingway's first months in Paris. The article describes the Café Rotonde which is located at the corner of the Boulevard Montparnasse and the Boulevard Raspail on the left bank of the Seine. Hemingway again describes the negative effect of tourism in Paris and regards himself as a true hard-working writer as opposed to the visitors of the Café Rotonde.

Although the left bank of the Seine is known to be the side for artists, Hemingway describes a crowd of people who only pretend to be artists: "[…] they insist upon posing as artists." (Hemingway, "American Bohemians"). He not only says that these people are pretenders but calls them *scum*:

> The scum of Greenwhich Village, New York […] New scum, of course, has risen to take place of the old, but the oldest scum, the thickest scum and the scummiest scum has come across the ocean […]. (ibid.)

This excessive repetition of the word *scum* strengthens Hemingway's attitude towards the crowd at the Café Rotonde right from the start. He concludes his first paragraph by stating the place is a: "[…] showplace for tourists in search of atmosphere." (ibid.). Moreover, the author describes two individuals of the crowd. The first one being a painter who admires her own work, but the reader gets to know that her painting is only one of "[...] some 3,000 others […]" (ibid.). Therefore, she is not an extraordinary artist, but only a woman desperate to become one. The second group of individuals are three men drinking at the cost of an older woman. Hemingway connotates this negatively, as a man should pay for himself. This part is typically contradictory for Hemingway, as he was mainly

14

living at the expanse of his wife Hadley during that time: "They did not need Hemingway's income from *Star* feature stories, for Hadley's several trust funds provided them with almost $3000 a year, more than enough money to live well in Paris." (Reynolds, *Hemingway* 5). Still, he wants to maintain the importance of being a hard-working man to become a successful artist.

Hemingway describes the Café Rotonde as a place where people meet to be individual and different, but which results into a "[…] uniformity of eccentricity." (Hemingway, "American Bohemians"). He wants to warn true artists and to remind them that "[…] there has not been much good poetry written in cafés." (ibid.). Nevertheless, this article shows the permissiveness of Paris and its freedom, i.e. regarding the excessive usage of alcohol.

5. Conclusion

The Paris of the 1920's is a permissive city dominated by freedom of all kinds. It stands in contrast with all values of America during that time, as life in America was puritan and conventional. The lack of support for artists and the longing for a life in freedom are the main reasons for the mass expatriation to Paris in the 1920's. Artists believed to only be able to write truly and creatively in the European city. They felt imprisoned in America. In addition, life in Paris means life in excess regarding alcohol and sexuality, as these were the most prohibited actions in America during that time. Also, Hemingway's way to Paris was a typical one. He was one of many expatriates and had the luck of an easy and quick acclimatization. Furthermore, the author had no worries when it comes to money due to his writings for the Toronto *Star* and especially due to his wife Hadley as she was financially stable.

Hemingway portrays Paris in his writings in much detail. *The Sun Also Rises* describes the city geographically as well as its lifestyle. Countless walks and taxi rides through the city establish a guidebook for Parisian lifestyle. It includes much alcohol and sexual desire. *A Moveable Feast* offers less geographical descriptions but more psychological ones. Here, Paris is depicted as a city in which one can become a successful artist. Its numerous restaurants and cafés support the cycle of hunger and creativity and the freedom of sexuality brighten the artist's mind. Lastly, Hemingway's works of journalism represent the city in different perspectives. Whereas his article "Living on $1,000 a Year in Paris" shows how a life in Paris can be comfortable and cheap, the article "American Bohemians in Paris" highlight the danger of tourism. A person who wants to become a

15

true artist must delimit oneself from tourists. He/she must engage him-/herself fully as a Parisian.

Overall, Hemingway portrays Paris as a permissive city with infinite possibilities for artists. Although his descriptions dominate the Left Bank of the Seine, he still manages to create an image of the city as a whole.

Bibliography

Primary Literature

Hemingway, Ernest. "American Bohemians in Paris" *Dateline: Toronto. The complete Toronto Star Dispatches, 1920-1924*, edited by William First Scribner eBook edition, 2002.

Hemingway, Ernest. *A Moveable Feast*. London: Arrow Books, 2011.

Hemingway, Ernest. "Living on $1,000 a Year in Paris." *Dateline: Toronto. The complete Toronto Star Dispatches, 1920-1924*, edited by William First Scribner eBook edition, 2002.

Hemingway, Ernest. *The Sun Also Rises.* Scribner, 2006.

Secondary Literature

Aldridge, John W. "Afterthoughts on the Twenties and *The Sun Also Rises*." *New Essay in The Sun Also Rises,* edited by Linda Wagner-Martin. Cambridge University Press, 1987, pp. 109-129.

Caswell, Claude. "City Of Brotherly Love: The Influence Of Paris And Prostitution On Hemingway's Fiction." *French Connections: Hemingway and Fitzgerald Abroad*, edited by J. Gerald Kennedy and Jackson R. Bryer. Macmillan, 1998, pp. 75-100.

Daufenbach, Claus. " ‚The vast bright Babylon': Die amerikanischen Expatriates im Paris der Zwanziger Jahre." *Begegnung zweier Kontinente,* edited by Ralph Dietl, et al. WVT Wissenschaftlicher Verlag Trier, 1999, pp. 291-303,

De Roche, Linda. *The Jazz Age: A Historical Exploration of Literature*, ABC-CLIO, LLC, 2015. ProQuest Ebook Central, https://ebookcentral.proquest.com/lib/ulb-bonn/detail.action?docID=4002900.

Donaldson, Scott. "Humor in The Sun Also Rises." *New Essay in The Sun Also Rises,* edited by Linda Wagner-Martin. Cambridge University Press, 1987, pp. 19-41.

Earnest, Ernest. *Expatriates and Patriots: American artists, scholars, and writers in Europe.* Duke University Press, 1968.

Fabre, Michael. *From Harlem to Paris: Black American Writers in France, 1840 – 1980.* University of Illinois, 1991.

Field, Allyson Nadja. "Expatriate Lifestyle as Tourist Destination: The Sun Also Rises and Experiential Travelogues of the Twenties." *The Hemingway Review,* Volume 25, Number 2, Spring 2006, pp. 29-43.

Griffin, Peter. *Less Than a Treason: Hemingway in Paris.* Oxford University Press, 1990.

Kennedy, Gerald J. *Imagining Paris: Exile, Writing, and American Identity.* Yale University Press, 1993.

"Lost Generation." Britannica Academic, Encyclopædia Britannica, 27 Nov. 2019. academic.eb.com/levels/collegiate/article/Lost-Generation/49008. Accessed 14 Aug. 2020.

Martin, Robert A. "The Expatriate Predicament In *The Sun Also Rises.*" *French Connections: Hemingway and Fitzgerald Abroad,* edited by J. Gerald Kennedy and Jackson R. Bryer. Macmillan, 1998, pp. 61-73.

Martin, Wendy. "Brett Ashley as New Woman in *The Sun Also Rises.*" *New Essay in The Sun Also Rises,* edited by Linda Wagner-Martin. Cambridge University Press, 1987, pp. 65-82.

Pizer, Donald. *American Expatriate Writing and the Paris Moment: Modernism and Place.* Louisiana State University Press, 1996.

Reynolds, Michael. *Hemingway: The Paris Years.* Basil Blackwell Ltd, 1989.

Reynolds, Michael. *The Young Hemingway.* London: Blackwell Publishers 1986.

Reynolds, Michael S. "The *Sun* in Its Time: Recovering the Historical Context." *New Essay in The Sun Also Rises,* edited by Linda Wagner-Martin. Cambridge University Press, 1987, pp. 43-64.

Stoneback, H. R. "'Very Cheerful and clean and sane and lovely': Hemingway's 'very pleasant land of France'." *French Connections: Hemingway and Fitzgerald Abroad,* edited by J. Gerald Kennedy and Jackson R. Bryer. Macmillan, 1998, pp. 33-59.

Wagner-Martin, Linda. *New Essays on The Sun Also Rises.* Cambridge University Press, 1987.